DIESEL AND ELECTRIC TRAINS
A NEW ERA OF RAILWAYS

DAVID REED

AMBERLEY

To my friend and colleague of many years John Dawson for encouraging me to have the pictures published, also for planning the many trips we have made together, both in years gone by and which we still enjoy in retirement.

First published 2022

Amberley Publishing
The Hill, Stroud
Gloucestershire, GL5 4EP

www.amberley-books.com

Copyright © David Reed, 2022

The right of David Reed to be identified as the Author of this work has been asserted in accordance with the Copyrights, Designs and Patents Act 1988.

ISBN 978 1 3981 0995 7 (print)
ISBN 978 1 3981 0996 4 (ebook)

British Library Cataloguing in Publication Data. A catalogue record for this book is available from the British Library.

Typesetting by SJmagic DESIGN SERVICES, India.
Printed in Great Britain.

Introduction

This volume follows on from my first book *Steam Railways: Final Operations in the Southern Region and the Early Preservation Years* and illustrates my memories of what became in the 1960s and 1970s a new era of diesel and electric trains.

My earliest pictures were taken from 1967 onwards when I was a teenager studying for my GCE O level exams, during which time I was primarily taking photographs of steam trains at Basingstoke and elsewhere. These photographs of diesel and electric trains were initially taken with a very basic Purma Plus camera I borrowed from my mother. However when I started work in the 1970s I was able to afford a 35 mm single lens reflex camera. This was only a fairly ordinary Zenith B instrument made in Russia but gave me greater flexibility in shutter speed and lens aperture settings. A Philips exposure calculator enabled me to assess the light conditions and select the right lens aperture and shutter speed until I obtained a small Yashica clip-on exposure meter.

British Rail used to run several training schemes for school leavers and graduates in a variety of commercial, operating and engineering disciplines. In September 1970, with ten other school leavers with whom I still keep in touch, I joined the Railway Studentship Training Scheme that provided training in operating and commercial aspects of the railway. We were encouraged to get out and about on the trains to observe the railway at work and some of us used to meet up at weekends and go travelling. As well as having only a very ordinary camera, I did not have any special access to the railway lineside, nor access by car, to take my photographs. All the pictures were taken from station platforms and other publicly accessible places in the course of my train journeys. So my colour slides of diesel and electric trains are effectively my souvenir records of those and other trips, taken much in the manner of holiday photographs.

In this book you will initially be taken around the London Midland and Eastern regions, followed by the Scottish and Western regions of British Rail. The photographs date from 1967 through to the 1970s with some trains appearing in the original green and maroon liveries and many in the later corporate Rail Blue. The pictures embrace mundane multiple units as well as the main line locomotive-hauled trains of the time. Almost all the traction types depicted are no longer in regular service and many only exist in preservation at heritage railway sites or hauling main line excursion trains.

A period of considerable change on Britain's railways is covered by this book, as a new era of modern, clean, fast and efficient diesel and electric trains developed. It is easy to forget that the first diesel and electric locomotives hauled dull maroon carriages just as steam locos had. The change to the corporate image Rail Blue colour for locomotives signified a new era, that of a market-led railway. The yellow front ends, primarily for the safety of track maintenance workers, also helped to add a modern look to the trains. I believe it was the late Cyril Freezer, who when editor of the *Railway Modeller* magazine, coined the term 'Modern Image' and encouraged the modelling of and interest in diesel and electric trains in the 1960s. Express train carriages were painted in blue and grey livery and other suburban and local trains in plain blue, which signified a complete break with the historical and regional colours previously used.

Not only the livery colours but the labelling of trains and stations was modernised by adoption of the British Rail Corporate Identity in 1964. The Rail Alphabet lettering format and the 'Double Arrow' corporate symbol were part of a complete design makeover introduced to mould all the various historical and regional strands of the railway into one company. A Corporate Identity manual was issued in 1965, which assisted staff in the application of the identity to every aspect of the railway from station signs, train liveries and lineside notices to timetables and publicity material. This culminated in what was probably the most significant change of all, the adoption of the 'Inter-City' brand for express trains. The double arrow symbol and the 'InterCity' brand (the hyphen was later dropped) continue to be instantly recognisable.

Forgive me for being old fashioned in this book if I refer to locomotives and multiple units by their earlier Type number, Class name and other designations of the time. I feel this helps to keep the book in its historical context and relates better to the 'D' and 'E' number prefixes the diesel and electric locomotives originally carried. The later TOPS (Total Operations Processing System) computer-based classification and numbering for trains falls outside the timeframe of this book, and similarly, there will be few pictures featuring air-conditioned trains.

When many of these pictures were taken the corporate image was still being implemented so in some photographs you will see reliveried blue locomotives and multiple units and blue and grey trains operating alongside the old regional station signage colours.

With one exception, all the pictures in this book were taken by me and none have been previously published. Being primarily interested in taking souvenir photographs, I didn't always keep detailed records of the locomotives, locations and dates, etc., so please forgive the occasional omissions and errors of memory.

I must thank my wife, Margaret, for her patience and support during the preparation of this book and for checking my manuscript. Thanks are also due to my friend and colleague of many years John Dawson for encouraging me to have the pictures published, also for reading through my text and suggesting many changes and additions. I also thank John for planning the various trips we have made, both in years gone by, and which we still enjoy undertaking in retirement.

Although some people may regard the corporate image blue and grey period as monotonous and dull, it was a very interesting period to experience as British Railways dragged itself into the new era of modern British Rail.

Part 1 Eastern and London Midland Regions

My first sighting of modern West Coast electric traction was at a very wet Euston station in the late 1960s. We see one of the early AL series electric locomotives on the left alongside an AL6 on a Glasgow service. The AL6 is in Electric Blue (a different shade to the later Rail Blue) with small yellow warning panel and white cab window surround, the livery I felt best suited these locos. Parcels are being loaded into the brake van from a BRUTE (British Railways Utility Trolley Equipment), an everyday occurrence at this time.

On the same occasion an English Electric Type 1 Bo-Bo diesel, D8003, is stabled in the wet at Euston. It is in green livery with small yellow warning panels and with headcode discs. At the time I was excited to see this loco, as I owned one of the Hornby Dublo 00 scale models.

A Brush Type 4 and English Electric Type 5 Deltic diesel, both in green livery with small yellow warning panels, are seen at Kings Cross. The Deltic is emerging from Gasworks Tunnel hauling a train composed largely of blue-and-grey coaching stock, with one early Mark 2a maroon integrally constructed FK (corridor first) carriage. The Southern Region also had some of these Mark 2a FKs in green livery.

With the arch of St Pancras station looming in the background, a bevy of Brush Type 2 diesels line up with their Class 2 commuter departures on the suburban side of Kings Cross station. The locos are all in green livery and just one had received an all-over yellow front. They are all at the head of trains comprising Mark 1 non-gangwayed suburban carriages. 'Thameslink' and the general electrification and modernisation of north London suburban services were still some time in the future.

The diesel stabling and refuelling point at Kings Cross hosts two English Electric Deltic diesel locos, one each in green and Rail Blue, with a third, rather dirty specimen, shunting. The Deltics were introduced in 1961 and at the time were the most powerful and fastest diesel locomotives in the UK.

This picture is believed to be of D9015 *Tulyar* arriving at Kings Cross with a train of Metro-Cammell Mark 1 Pullman coaches in umber and cream and a Mark 1 maroon full brake van. The Deltic loco still carries its lovely two-tone green livery and white cab window surrounds, but with the later yellow nose. Note the absence of orange vests for the track maintenance staff.

An English Electric Co-Co Type 3, D6714, built in 1961, takes a rest in Liverpool Street station. She was built at the Vulcan Foundry and initially allocated to Stratford depot. Here she wears green livery with twin headcode boxes and full yellow nose ends. At this time the redevelopment of Liverpool Street station was still years away.

Around the time this photograph was taken, St Pancras station was slated for closure under route rationalisation proposals and may even have become a transport museum. The station looks somewhat different now with Eurostar trains and shops in the undercroft. Here a Type 4 Peak Class 1-Co-Co-1 diesel locomotive introduced by BR in 1959, is waiting to head north to Leeds.

Peak diesel loco D167, built in 1961, emerges from the gloom as she shunts away from the buffers at St Pancras station. She is wearing extremely dirty original green livery with small yellow warning panel, but someone has obviously been at work with a paintbrush or cleaning rag to brighten up the bufferbeam.

The green cab of Peak D40, with the St Pancras signal cabin behind, provides a contrast with the corporate blue livery of her sister engine seen arriving at St Pancras with a train from the Midlands.

On a family holiday to North Wales in August 1967 we called at Holyhead where I chanced to take this picture inside the station. I still remember this loco more by name than number, it being *Aquitania*, D215. An English Electric Type 4 1-Co-Co-1 introduced in 1958, she is still in green livery with her nameplates in place.

With the limestone lions standing guard, a Park Royal Diesel Multiple Unit (DMU) in green livery disappears into the darkness of the Britannia Tubular Bridge in August 1967. The foundation stone was laid in 1846 and it allowed the Chester and Holyhead Railway to cross the Menai Strait, facilitating a through service to Ireland by train and ship.

Type 4 traction at Crewe Works. Beside the traverser, a freshly outshopped Brush Type 4 and a more workstained English Electric Type 4 stand at Crewe Works in various stages of overhaul. The following pictures of Crewe Works were taken while I was on a training course at Crewe in autumn 1970.

A Brush Type 4, which looks as though it is en route to the paint shop, is escorted on the traverser by an English Electric 350 hp diesel shunter. At its zenith over 20,000 people were employed at Crewe Works.

An interesting mix of motive power. A Metro-Cammell DMU approaches en route to Chester, while in the works yard an English Electric Type 1, a Brush Type 4 and a Southern Region 1,600 hp Bo-Bo electro-diesel are on test.

A six-car Trans-Pennine DMU, introduced in 1960 and built at Swindon, emerges from Edge Hill cutting as it arrives at Liverpool Lime Street station. Surely this was the most attractive of the British Railways multiple-unit designs? It must certainly rival the Glasgow Blue Trains for first place.

Despite being covered in a uniform layer of dirt, AL6 electric loco no. E3143 draws admiring glances from a couple of young enthusiasts at Birmingham New Street station while awaiting departure south to Euston. An AM10 EMU (Electric Multiple Unit) can be glimpsed in the background.

A Peak diesel-electric loco, believed to be no. 89 *Honourable Artillery Company* waits with the northbound Thames-Clyde Express service at Carlisle. She still carries her split headcode boxes and there is evidence of leakage from the steam heating pipes at the front and rear of the loco. Many early diesel locos were fitted with train heating boilers to warm the older steam-heated carriages.

English Electric Type 4 D236 in green livery and yellow nose waits at Carlisle with a parcels train. The front end connecting doors and headcode discs are evident.

English Electric 2,700 hp diesel D446 is ready to head southbound from Carlisle with an afternoon service to Euston. These locos were built at the Vulcan Foundry, Newton-le-Willows, Lancashire, from 1967 onwards and used primarily on the London Midland Region Anglo-Scottish trains. Following electrification northwards from Weaver Junction, just north of Crewe, and introduction of the Electric Scots services to Glasgow in 1974, she moved to the Western Region where she was later named *Ajax*.

A DMU waits at North Woolwich, later to become the eastern terminus of the North London Line, with the cranes of London's Royal Docks in the background. Diesel traction replaced steam on this line in 1963 but more recently transport in this area has been revolutionised by the development of the Docklands Light Railway and London City Airport.

A Swindon-built Cross Country DMU on a Birmingham New Street to Norwich train approaches Thetford. Very spick and span in clean blue and grey livery, it is passing the Great Eastern Railway signal box.

Brush Type 2 D5566 passes through Thetford station on 5 June 1971, hauling a Great Yarmouth to Newcastle train.

Two DMUs cross the Halvergate Marshes next to Breydon Water en route from Norwich to Great Yarmouth via Berney Arms.

Another Brush Type 2, this time D5692, passes through Reedham station on a Leeds to Great Yarmouth service also on 5 June 1971. The service was booked to go via Acle so was probably diverted on this occasion.

On the same date, 5 June, passengers make ready to board as a Cravens DMU, introduced in 1956, arrives at Reedham on a Norwich to Lowestoft working.

A smartly turned out driver, with brake handle in hand, boards a Gloucester Railway Carriage & Wagon Co. twin unit at Lowestoft in the spring of 1971. The unit will form a service to Ipswich.

Forgive the rays from the platform lights but I like the atmosphere. A 6 second time exposure features no. D5027 and a DMU at Shrewsbury.

A DMU is loaded with parcels and mail at Shrewsbury. Several BRUTE and mail trolleys are evident. At this time so much in the way of parcels and mail used to be conveyed by passenger trains that station dwell times had to allow for loading and unloading.

On a damp 27 November 1971 green Brush Type 4 D1974 sits at the head of the 09.10 Kings Cross to Leeds and Hull service. The train crew seem to be exchanging pleasantries, maybe lamenting the weather, prior to departure.

A train of clean blue Birmingham RC&W Co. DMUs sits in the cavernous shell of Bradford Exchange station on 27 November 1971. Note the enormous water column upright at the end of the platform. The station was originally opened jointly by the Lancashire & Yorkshire and Great Northern railways in 1850.

A Sulzer Type 2, D5175, awaits departure from Bradford Forster Square station at the head of a train of parcels stock. Built by the Midland Railway in 1890 with an overall roof, this station and the services using it were rationalised following the Beeching cuts in the 1960s.

A line of Corinthian columns stand sentry on the platform and semaphore signals stand guard at the platform end at Bradford Exchange as a DMU departs. Around 1973 the station, with its ten platforms, was demolished and the site now hosts the Bradford Crown Court. A new, smaller station was built on another site and when a bus terminal was opened alongside it was renamed Bradford Interchange.

A Metro-Cammell DMU sits in a rather run-down Ilkley station. Note the orange-coloured station nameplates, this being the identifying colour for the North Eastern Region of British Railways. Ilkley is reputed to be the last station lit by gas, this finally being turned off in the 1980s.

A night shot of an English Electric Type 4 believed to be at a rather damp Leeds station. I have always been intrigued by the contrast between the warm yellowish glow of the incandescent bulbs in the driver's cab with the cool whiteness of the station fluorescent lighting all around.

The next few photographs illustrate a journey from London to visit the Sudbury branch on Saturday 4 March 1972. Here we see two EMUs, Liverpool Street to Shenfield Class AM6 no. 043 and Great Eastern Outer Suburban Class AM7 no. 132 awaiting the start of their journeys from Liverpool Street station. The AM6 units had open saloons and sliding entry doors while the AM7 units were basically BR standard non-gangwayed slam-door carriages.

An AM9 Liverpool Street to Clacton and Walton express EMU awaits departure from London Liverpool Street station. They were previously painted in BR lined maroon with a small yellow warning panel within the corridor gangway. At this time, although repainted in corporate blue and grey livery, the driving cabs still retained their stylish wraparound windows.

A train of AM9 Liverpool Street to Clacton and Walton units has arrived at one of their namesake stations, Clacton. The wraparound cab windows were later replaced with flat toughened glass windscreens to resist missiles thrown by vandals.

The corporate image blue livery is seen here at its very best. Beautifully turned out Brush Type 4 diesel D1563 and its equally well turned out train of Mark 1 carriages is seen at Colchester station en route to Norwich on 4 March 1972. These locos were built at the Falcon Works of Brush Traction in Loughborough and at the British Railways works at Crewe.

The same train, complete with tail lamp, heads east from Colchester. It is passing through a tunnel of overhead catenary masts and headspans, foreshortened by a telephoto lens, as it continues towards Ipswich and Norwich.

Brush Type 4 D1528 at the head of a Norwich to Liverpool Street train slows on arrival at Colchester.

A Metro-Cammell and Cravens two-car DMU has arrived at Sudbury station on 4 March 1972. Following the Beeching cuts the line from Marks Tey to Cambridge, known as the Stour Valley route, was truncated at Sudbury in March 1967. Note the dark blue Sudbury station sign, this being the regional colour for Eastern Region signage.

The Cravens and Metro-Cammell DMU is ready to leave Sudbury to return to Marks Tey on the same date, 4 March 1972. Sudbury station became unstaffed in 1966 when the East Anglia Paytrain Network was established and all tickets were then issued and checked on board the trains.

The Metro-Cammell DMU makes a contrast with the ornate platform canopy bracket at Sudbury, also on 4 March. When Sudbury became a single line terminus in 1967 the footbridge seen in the background was no longer required. It has since been moved to the East Anglian Railway Museum at Chappell & Wakes Colne, where it facilitates safe access across the running lines to the museum.

At Marks Tey station, junction for the Sudbury branch, a Brush Type 4 diesel rushes through with a container train to Felixstowe. British Rail was at the forefront of the container revolution with its introduction of the 'Liner Train' concept, later marketed as Freightliner.

Viewed from an elevated position on the footbridge at Marks Tey, passengers make ready to board an AM9 Clacton electric unit as it arrives with a service to London Liverpool Street.

Under a veritable cocoon of overhead equipment, another Brush Type 4, D1525 approaches Shenfield on an express to Liverpool Street.

An AM7 outer-suburban four-car EMU, no. 125, pauses at Shenfield with a service for Southend.

A time exposure of around 6 seconds sees two AM2 EMUs take an evening rest at the end of their journeys at Fenchurch Street station on Saturday 4 March 1972.

One of the later series of Peak class diesel locomotives, D166, draws its northbound Midland Main Line service, the 'Thames-Clyde Express', into Leicester on 31 March 1972. The 'Thames-Clyde Express' originally ran between St Pancras and Glasgow St Enoch until the latter station closed in 1966 and it operated instead to Glasgow Central.

D5024 rests beneath the gables of the massive train shed at Manchester Victoria on 31 March 1972. Platform 11, from which this picture was taken, was joined up to Manchester Exchange station in 1929 and created Europe's longest platform at 2,238 feet. Crossovers enabled three trains to be accommodated and to arrive and depart simultaneously.

As three generations of passengers walk down the platform together, a DMU sits awaiting departure time at Chester on a Runcorn service. Maroon London Midland Region station signage is still well in evidence here. Crewe station opened in 1837 on the Grand Junction Railway, which later became part of the London North Western Railway, subsequently incorporated into the London Midland & Scottish Railway.

A Liverpool to Southport line 630 volt DC 3rd rail EMU (with Motor Open Brake Second M28361M leading) awaits departure from Liverpool Exchange station in 1972. The station opened in 1850, serving the Lancashire & Yorkshire and East Lancashire Railways and services were electrified in 1904. Following bomb damage during the Second World War, the roof of Liverpool Exchange station was never fully repaired and after diversion of services through the Merseyrail tunnels in the 1970s the station closed.

The driver and an enthusiast with his young son exchange pleasantries. Meanwhile diesel shunter D3791 takes a break at the head of a short rake of parcels vans in one of the bay platforms at Wigan North Western station on 1 April 1972.

One of the English Electric Type 5 diesel locos, D442 speeds towards Wigan North Western station on a Blackpool North to Euston service on 1 April 1972. The overhead lines are still being installed ready for operation of the 'Electric Scots' between Euston and Glasgow. Later transferred to the Western Region and named *Triumph*, D442 was withdrawn in 1990 and is now preserved.

In contrast we see here a Derby Works-built DMU (driving trailer M56271 leading) entering Warrington Central station on 1 April 1972. Warrington Central was opened in the 1870s and is on the former Cheshire Lines Committee route between Liverpool and Manchester. Unlike Warrington Bank Quay on the West Coast Main Line, it is still served by diesel trains.

Also on 1 April 1972, Altrincham station echoes to the throb of a Sulzer diesel engine as BR Type 2 locomotive D7543, built in 1965 and still in green livery, drifts through with a train of hopper wagons. The original Manchester, South Junction & Altrincham Railway station was opened in 1881, and Manchester Metrolink trams now serve this station.

English Electric Type 4 D217 *Carinthia* in green livery and still carrying its nameplate, arrives at Chester General station. The refreshment trolley is being readied to join this train by its white-coated attendant. Built in 1959, 2,000 hp *Carinthia* was named after the Cunard liner in 1962.

The signal is clear for a DMU leaving Chester General heading towards Runcorn, as it passes in the shadow of Chester No. 2 signal box. The station dates from the 1840s, being extended in the 1870s to accommodate increasing traffic. It was served by Great Western Railway services from Birkenhead Woodside to Shrewsbury, Wolverhampton Low Level, Birmingham Snow Hill and Paddington.

A Wirral & Mersey EMU passes Rock Ferry signal box. It is making its way up the former Great Western and London North Western Railway Joint Line on the Wirral towards Birkenhead and Liverpool. Rock Ferry station opened in 1862 and was also situated on the Great Western Railway route from Birkenhead Woodside to Paddington. In 1891 Rock Ferry became an interchange with the Mersey Railway and the local services were electrified in 1903.

A contrast in diesel and electric multiple units as an AM3 Wirral & Mersey 650 volt DC 3rd rail EMU (with Motor Open Brake Second M28685M leading) is seen at Rock Ferry station. Originally an LMS design dating from 1938, a further batch of AM3 units was built by British Railways in 1956. Emergency end doors for tunnel operation were fitted in 1972 and a set was preserved in LMS maroon livery in 1985.

In the shadow of the trainshed roof, D414 waits to leave Preston with a northbound express from Liverpool to Glasgow Central on 2 April 1972. Built in 1968 she was later transferred to the Western Region, where in 1978 she was named *Warspite*.

1960s motive power in 1970s liveries lined up under the overall roof at Liverpool Lime Street station on 3 April 1972 at 10.39. A London Midland Region Western Lines 25kV AC 4 car EMU is seen on the left with a couple of AL6 electric locos and a DMU.

A minute later, the less environmentally friendly aspects of first generation DMUs is shown here at Liverpool Lime Street as an exhaust haze drifts up into the roof.

While an AL6 electric loco E3107 awaits departure southbound, a DMU emerges from Edge Hill cutting and tunnel into Liverpool Lime Street station, also on 3 April 1972. Lime Street station opened in 1836, reached by tunnels from the previous station at Edge Hill, and originally served the Liverpool & Manchester and Grand Junction railways.

A Derby Works-built two-car DMU (with Motor Composite M52064 leading) waits departure from Southport for Liverpool Lime Street on 3 April 1972. At this time, before the Merseyrail link under Liverpool was constructed, about four trains daily ran direct to Lime Street to offer easier interchange with Inter-City services.

A very clean and pristine Birmingham RC&W Co. three-car set (with Motor Brake Second M50434 leading) is ready to leave Manchester Piccadilly station with a Buxton service. Bright red bufferbeams look very colourful but I don't think they were the norm with corporate blue livery and yellow front ends!

On 3 April 1972 Peak class D46 is waiting to leave Manchester Piccadilly on the midday departure to St Pancras. D46 was built at Crewe works in 1961. Piccadilly station first opened as Store Street in 1842, became Manchester London Road in 1847 and following the modernisation of the West Coast Main Line was renamed Manchester Piccadilly in 1960.

A Manchester–Hadfield–Glossop EMU operating on 1,500 volts DC (with Driving Trailer Open Second M59607M leading) approaches Dinting station on 3 April 1972.

Crossing Dinting Viaduct on 3 April 1972 is another Manchester–Hadfield–Glossop unit. Dinting and its smaller sister, Etherow Viaduct, were originally built of stone piers with timber spans in the 1840s, the wrought-iron plate girders being installed to replace the timber in 1859. Due to the increasing tonnage of coal conveyed on the line, the original wrought ironwork was strengthened in 1919 by the construction of intermediate brick pillars, unevenly spaced due to a road and stream in the valley below.

Through the footbridge metalwork at Dinting Lane Crossing, with the crossing-keeper's cottage on the right, is another Manchester–Hadfield–Glossop EMU (with Driving Trailer Open Second M59605M leading). Electrification of the Woodhead Line was first mooted by the Great Central Railway before the First World War and later by the London North Eastern Railway, but delayed by the Second World War, and eventually completed by British Railways in 1955. These trains were withdrawn in the 1980s when the local lines were modernised and converted to 25kV AC.

As the smart traincrew member strides purposefully towards me, a Cravens two-car DMU introduced in 1957 (with Motor Brake Second M50779 towards the camera) is waiting at Bury Bolton Street station on 3 April 1972. Opened in 1846, this station is now home to the East Lancashire Railway heritage line and a new terminal served by Metrolink trams has been built closer to the town centre.

The former steam shed at Bury closed in 1965, but became host to a number of stored locomotives. The prototype Woodhead Line EM1 Bo-Bo electric locomotive, E26000 *Tommy*, is on the right. *Tommy* was built in 1941 by the London North Eastern Railway but completion of the electrification was delayed by the Second World War. The loco was shipped to Holland for use on the Dutch Railways where the name was given. Other more modern West Coast AL series electric locos are stored on the left and following modification to their rectifiers these later re-entered service.

On 12 May 1973 a bevy of Brush Type 4 locos has brought 'Merrymaker' excursion trains to Spalding. The Flower Festival was in full swing and the Southern Region of BR operated two 'Pleasure Seeker' excursion trains to the event. One was loco-hauled from the South Eastern Division and the other, from the Central Division, used two 6B Hastings Line straight-sided Diesel-Electric Multiple Units (DEMUs), in the window of which a Brush diesel is reflected.

Hastings Line narrow-bodied 6B DEMU no. 1033 leads the return Southern Region Central Division 'Pleasure Seeker' excursion at Spalding on 12 May 1973. The narrow bodies were necessitated by the limited clearances in certain tunnels between Tonbridge and Hastings. This outward excursion started from Hastings and picked up passengers from Eastbourne, Lewes, then Brighton main line and connecting stations.

On the same date English Electric Type 4 D253 is ticking over at the head of the return Southern Region South Eastern Division 'Pleasure Seeker' train at Spalding, about to head back to Kent with changes of motive power en route.

Following electrification from Weaver Junction to Glasgow in the early 1970s the Class 87 locos were introduced to haul the Electric Scot services from Euston. The author, very much younger than now, is seen in this picture taken by my brother, Roger Reed, with no. 87023 at Euston en route to a family wedding. No. 87023 entered service in 1974, was named *Highland Chieftain* in 1978 (the name previously carried by A2 Pacific no. 60507), and was exported to Bulgaria in 2012.

Part 2 Scottish Region

Ready to speed north to Scotland is a pristine Type 5 English Electric Deltic no. 9000 *Royal Scots Grey*. She is warming up at Kings Cross at the head of the 10.00 'Flying Scotsman' service to Edinburgh on 16 November 1972 with a train of air-conditioned Mark 2 coaching stock.

Sulzer Type 2 diesel no. 5364 is ready to depart from Mallaig on 11 September 1971 with the 14.05 service to Glasgow conveying a Buffet-Restaurant Car. I recall that on one journey from London to Mallaig in the late 1960s I had the pleasure of a sleeping car from London and later walked through to the restaurant car for a full silver-service breakfast. Those were the days!

On the same date, 11 September, with the 14.05 Glasgow service on the left, a Type 2 is heading the train on the right to Fort William. Notice on the left a Mallaig station sign in the light blue regional colour of the Scottish Region.

Here we are passing over the famous Glenfinnan Viaduct situated at the head of Loch Shiel. The viaduct was built by 'Concrete Bob' McAlpine using unreinforced concrete as the local stone was too hard to work for masonry. It has twenty-one arches of 50 feet span, is 416 yards long and 100 feet high. To take account of any settlement there is a sliding steel joint at the head of each arch. The arches themselves are cylindrical and the curve was achieved by making the pillars wedge-shaped.

In the shadow of the mountains, Inverness depot is host to several Type 2 diesels, including no. 5371 in green in the foreground and behind it nos 5409 and 5362 in blue.

Quantities of parcels and mail are being loaded into a green-liveried Swindon-built three-car Cross Country DMU (Sc51794 nearest) at Inverness, capital of the Highlands. The station was opened in 1855 by the Inverness & Nairn Railway, and enlarged in 1857.

A classic view of Glasgow Central station on 12 September 1971 with AM3 Glasgow area Blue Train EMU no. 025 awaiting departure for Gourock. Introduced in the 1960s, they were originally painted in a striking Caledonian Blue livery. Although they were later repainted into Corporate Identity Rail Blue with all-yellow front ends as seen here, their wraparound cab windows still made them look elegant and modern.

A couple of three-car AM3 Blue Train sets, coincidentally 018 and 108, arrive at Port Glasgow station on 12 September 1971 as they form the 11.02 to Glasgow Central. The Scott Lithgow shipyard 'Goliath' crane, an echo of the area's glorious Clydebank shipbuilding past, towers over the area and dominates the background.

Also on 12 September 1971 Blue Train no. 103 sits among the floral displays at picturesque Wemyss Bay terminus station. This was built in 1903 for the Caledonian Railway and is the terminal for the ferry to Rothesay on the Isle of Bute. It is noted for the architectural design incorporating the use of curves and glass, the supporting ironwork seeming to sprout from the walls of the ticket office.

Another Blue Train, no. 044 is ready to leave Helensburgh Central station on 12 September for its run up the north bank of the Clyde valley to Bridgeton. Helensburgh Central opened in 1858 as the terminus of the Glasgow, Dumbarton & Helensburgh Railway, later absorbed into the North British Railway, and was rebuilt in 1897.

Passengers patiently await the departure of their 11.27 train from Stranraer to Glasgow on 13 September 1971. My original notes mention 'disenchanted passengers' and that there was a problem with the DMU. We see here the 'blunt' or inner end of a Swindon-built DMU.

On 13 September 1971, Sulzer Type 2 D5008 in green livery pauses at Stranraer on Loch Ryan. Maybe a Motive Power Inspector in suit and trilby is striding purposefully towards the loco as my notes state that the loco took us away 42 minutes late. D5008 was delivered from Derby in 1959. After allocations to the Southern and London Midland regions it was allocated to Eastfield in 1971 to allow withdrawal of Clayton Type 1 and North British Type 2 locos.

Later that day D5008 arrives at Ayr with a replacement train of loco-hauled stock. The station was opened in 1886 together with the large Station Hotel seen in the background. Despite being listed, the hotel fell into a state of disrepair and its future is uncertain. In mid-1959 D5008 underwent road tests with the London Midland Region Mobile Test Plant and the Dynamometer Car to assess the class. The results were published in a British Transport Commission Performance and Efficiency Test Bulletin.

DMU sets 124 and 146 in intermediate Rail Blue livery but with small yellow warning panel approach Kilwinning Junction en route to Largs on the Ayr coast on 13 September. Note the Ford Thames Trader lorry on the left, which would now be considered a classic vehicle.

On the same day, 13 September, passengers board another DMU, set 141 at Kilwinning on a service to Dalry.

Consecutively numbered British Railways Sulzer-engined Type 2 diesels D5126 and D5127 stand at the head of the 17.25 train from Glasgow Queen Street on 13 September 1971. The leading locomotive is fitted with the twin headlights provided to aid drivers operating on rural Highland Line services.

At Glasgow Queen Street station Birmingham RC&W Type 2 diesel loco no. 5412 is ready to depart for Edinburgh on the Glasgow–Edinburgh high-speed push-pull service on 13 September 1971. There would have been one of these diesel locomotives at each end of the rake of six Mark 2a coaches.

Another BRCW Type 2 in green livery and yellow front end, and still with its front end connecting doors, arrives at Glasgow Queen Street with a train of Mark 1 coaches in tow. This murky view is rather different today following the redevelopment of the Queen Street station area.

On a damp 14 September 1971 with low cloud covering the hills we see two more Type 2s at Achnasheen station. D5345 is heading the 10.30 Inverness to Kyle of Lochalsh service and awaits the arrival and passing of D5118 on an Inverness train.

A Sulzer-engined Type 2 awaits departure from Kyle of Lochalsh with a train of passenger coaches and vans. David MacBrayne's ferry *Loch Seaforth*, launched in 1947, is alongside the harbour having earlier been unloaded by the dockside crane. Some years later David Macbrayne, who also operated buses, would merge with the Caledonian Steam Packet Co. to become the well-known Caledonian-MacBrayne or Cal-Mac company.

In a scene that could well be from the nineteenth century, milk churns are loaded into the train at Dingwall station on 15 September 1971. A couple of English Electric Type 1 diesel locos are seen beyond the footbridge heading south past the signal box into the distance towards Inverness.

Sulzer Type 2 D5132, fitted with automatic token exchange apparatus in the cab-side recess, is seen in the shadows of the train shed on arrival at Thurso on 15 September 1971. Thurso station was opened in 1874 and is the northernmost station in Britain. It is also the nearest to the Scapa Flow naval base in the Orkneys. My father, who was in the Royal Navy, remembered with great interest travelling up to Thurso during the Second World War.

On the same day D5132 carries out some shunting at Thurso in order to retrieve the full brake coach from the buffer stops. A special purpose wagon can be seen in the goods yard. It is carrying a nuclear flask bound for Dounreay, where there was both a nuclear power station and a submarine nuclear plant testing facility.

Type 2 D5331 is seen from the footbridge as it arrives at Georgemas Junction from Wick on 15 September 1971. Georgemas Junction is where the Wick and Thurso lines meet and the train from Thurso can just be glimpsed on the left. Instead of the trains splitting and combining here at Georgemas Junction, they now run to Wick via Thurso.

A three-car Swindon-built Cross Country DMU has arrived at Aberdeen station from Inverness on 16 September 1971.

The driver and a member of the station staff exchange words as a very clean English Electric Type 4 D262 awaits its southbound departure from Aberdeen with the 12.30 train to Edinburgh on 16 September 1971.

A Metro-Cammell two-car DMU is berthed in Dundee Tay Bridge station on the same date, 16 September. The nearest carriage carries a rather faded intermediate blue livery with a small yellow warning panel.

D262 is heading our train on the approach spans to the Tay Bridge from the Dundee side. The foundation piers of the original bridge, which collapsed during a storm in 1879 sending a train plunging into the waters below, can be seen to the left of the new one. The 'new' bridge was constructed in 1887, the original girders from the first bridge being used where serviceable and it is one of the last great wrought-iron bridges.

By way of a contrast, here we are crossing the mighty Forth Bridge with a Metro-Cammell DMU approaching from the Edinburgh direction. The Forth Bridge company was formed in 1873 by the North British, the Midland and the Great Northern Railway companies. The three towers, 360 feet high, consist of steel tubes 12 feet in diameter and all the steelwork for the bridge was fabricated on site. Over 4,000 labourers were involved, 51,000 tons of steel were used and it was completed in 1890.

North Berwick station is host to Gloucester RC&W-built DMU (Motor Brake Second Sc 51109 leading) on the next departure back to Edinburgh on 17 September 1971. Note the single line token propped up in the cab window. The branch has an interesting recent history: dieselised in 1958, put up for closure under the Beeching Report and electrified in the 1990s.

On 17 September 1971 Sulzer Type 2 no. 5410 is seen following arrival at Edinburgh Waverley on the Glasgow–Edinburgh high-speed shuttle service.

At the other end of the same formation Type 2 no. 5387 is awaiting departure from Edinburgh on the 11.00 service back to Glasgow Queen Street. A rather ancient platform luggage trolley is in evidence on the right.

With parcels and mail carriages of mixed origins on the left, English Electric D418 edges gently into Carlisle Citadel station with a southbound service. So named because it is adjacent to the medieval fortress, Citadel station was opened in 1847 and is an important interchange between the West Coast main line, the Settle & Carlisle and Cumbrian Coast lines, the Newcastle–Carlisle line and the Glasgow & South Western route via Dumfries. D418 was later transferred to the Western Region and named *Resolution*.

An English Electric Type 4 no. 365 in charge of an Aberdeen to Glasgow train approaches Perth over the River Tay Bridge on 17 November 1972.

In a rather supernatural setting, Type 2 no. 5125 is seen looming out of bright sunlight at Perth station on 17 November 1972.

Frosty sleepers on the ground but hopefully warm sleepers in the Inter-City sleeping cars! A Cravens DMU passes a sleeping car train in the cavernous interior of Perth station on 18 November 1972. Perth was the junction where the North British Railway, the Caledonian Railway and the Highland Railway all met.

A Brush Type 4 and Metro-Cammell DMU are also seen at Perth station on 18 November 1972 following a light dusting of snow.

In bleak wintry conditions and under a very threatening grey sky, trains pass in the snow at Newtonmore, also on 18 November 1972. Newtonmore is nearly 70 miles from Perth and was opened in 1863.

Dumbarton station, which was opened in 1850, sees a Blue Train arriving en route for Balloch Pier on 19 November 1972.

On arrival at Balloch Pier the paddle steamer *Maid of the Loch* has steam up ready for a sailing on Loch Lomond. The *Maid of the Loch* was built by A & J Inglis of Glasgow and shipped in pieces by rail to Balloch for reassembly and launch in 1953. The *Maid* was withdrawn in 1981 but restoration is taking place. Balloch Pier station closed in 1986.

Part 3 Western Region

Maroon-liveried Western Region Warship class diesel hydraulic loco D812 *Royal Naval Reserve 1859-1959* arrives at Ilfracombe station on 2 August 1968. By this time the line had been rationalised and singled. The station was closed under the Beeching cuts on 5 October 1970.

For 4s 3d (about 21p in decimal currency) my brother and I travelled on this train from Ilfracombe to Barnstaple Town at the end of a family holiday. Where are these two young enthusiasts now? They seem quite enthralled as D812 draws over the level crossing and away from Barnstaple Town station.

A rather travel-stained Brush Type 4 diesel D1723 arrives at Paddington station. She entered traffic in 1964 and at some time in the future she carried the name *The Institution of Civil Engineers*.

A very work-stained D1046 *Western Marquis* in faded maroon livery with small yellow warning panel arrives at Reading General platform 4 with a service from Paddington on 7 November 1970. In the background the sign 'Alight here for Heathrow Airport' draws the attention of passengers to the Rail-Air coach link between Reading and Heathrow, providing a direct service to and from the airport.

On the same date a Swindon three-car Cross Country DMU (W50710 leading) sits in Taunton station yard waiting to form a train to Minehead.

Exeter Central station, previously known as Exeter Queen Street and once the hub of Southern Railway services to Devon and North Cornwall, is a shadow of its former self as a DMU arrives from Exmouth.

Portrait of a Western at Paddington. The Western Type 4 diesel hydraulic locos were perhaps the most iconic of all diesel locos with their modern angular design. They had a very high tractive effort of 72,600 lb and were the most powerful locos on the Western Region.

Southern Region 2HAL EMU 2641 sits at platform 4a at Reading General while a Brush Type 4 no. 1756 is ready to depart on its dash to Paddington. At this time the Southern Region only had this one platform to accommodate half-hourly trains to and from Waterloo and the hourly cross-country DEMU service to Guildford, Redhill, and Tonbridge.

With the landmark gasometers in the distance, a Western arrives at Reading General from Paddington.

A Western diesel hydraulic calls at Reading General en route to Paddington while a 4COR EMU arrives at Platform 4a on a Southern Region service from Waterloo.

Built at Swindon in 1963, an Inter-City DMU arrives at Reading General platform 4. The modern wraparound windows are seen to good effect. Originally intended for services between the south coast and south Wales, they were later used on outer-suburban services between Paddington, Newbury and Oxford, as seen here.

A bit of a hybrid here. As an express departs west, London area suburban unit no. 432 sits at Reading General platform 5 awaiting departure towards Paddington. The second coach is an additional Metro-Cammell centre car.

A trio of diesels sit at Exeter St David's stabling point. D868 *Zephyr* in atrocious external condition, a North British Type 2 D6334 with its spoked wheels visible, and an unidentified Brush Type 4.

A maroon Western diesel hydraulic has just arrived at Exeter St David's station and awaits departure westward. It is in the appalling external condition typical of so many Western Region locomotives at this time, reputedly due to the failure to properly rinse off the cleaning solution used in automatic washing plants.

Seen through a 25 mph speed restriction stencil, a Peak diesel electric arrives at Exeter St David's on a westward inter-regional working.

While passengers on the opposite platform 1 eagerly await the arrival of their westbound train, a DMU pauses in platform 3 at Exeter St David's station.

On the edge of Dartmoor, a DMU has arrived at Okehampton station on 19 December 1970 on the 13.55 service from Exeter St David's. This is the former Southern Railway route between Exeter and Plymouth and everything about the infrastructure says 'Southern'. Oh for a Bulleid Pacific steam locomotive and some green carriages to add the finishing touch.

A short distance along the old Southern Railway trackbed is Meldon trestle bridge and Meldon quarry. At this time the bridge was in use for lorry access to Meldon quarry, and the quarry still supplied high quality track ballast for the Southern and other regions.

A Hymek diesel hydraulic shunts from the platforms at Paddington. Another well-styled Western Region hydraulic loco class, D7036 is seen here in intermediate blue livery with small yellow warning panels and white cab window surrounds.

Brush Type 2 no. 5538 arrives at Paddington. The loco has headcode discs instead of a four-character headcode box above the cab, and still has the front connecting doors and bodyside footholds adjacent to the cab door.

With a haze of diesel exhaust drifting across the tracks, a grubby Western D1029 *Western Legionnaire* backs on to its train at Paddington.

A three-car Inter-City DMU is seen at Reading DMU depot. Another of these trains with its stylish wraparound windscreen can be seen in the right background.

The derelict London & South Western Railway signal box is front of scene on another visit to Meldon. A ballast brake van, with ploughs to spread the ballast across the track, is also visible together with ballast-loading hoppers and the shed for the quarry diesel shunter.

Meldon Viaduct, otherwise known as 'Bridge 613' on the former Southern Railway route to Plymouth. The viaduct was built in 1874, was doubled in 1879, and is effectively two parallel independent trestle bridges with their supporting legs interlaced.

Leaving the old turntable pit and shed yard on the left, a single-car DMU departs from Okehampton station towards Exeter. A nice 1960s Mini is parked on the loading dock on the right.

Warship diesel hydraulic D868 *Zephyr* waits to leave Exeter St David's station for Salisbury and Waterloo. The leading carriages are carrying the short-lived black-on-yellow bodyside destination boards showing 'Waterloo Salisbury Exeter', which were believed to be easier for passengers to read than roof-boards – and no doubt easier for staff to change.

The quarry's 350 hp diesel electric shunter at home in its shed at Meldon.

In green livery with yellow front end and cab window surrounds, a Hymek diesel hydraulic loco waits at Exeter St David's with a short train of six-wheeled glass-lined milk tankers in tow. At this time milk was still being collected from Torrington and Hemyock. Following the demise of steam traction, the loco number reads 7014, the 'D' having been painted out. The milk tankers would each hold around 3,000 gallons and the loaded tankers weighed about 25 tons each, as much as a bogie coach.

A DMU has just arrived from Paignton at Kingswear station. Kingswear station opened in 1864 and served Dartmouth via a ferry service across the river. It has an unusual train shed shown in the photograph. The branch is now somewhat busier than it is here, being a heritage line operated by the Torbay Steam Railway.

Leaving a haze of exhaust behind, a pristine Cross Country DMU departs from Bath Spa station. Note the signal box in its elevated position above the platform canopy. The station opened in 1840 and was renamed Bath Spa in the 1940s to distinguish it from the Somerset & Dorset Railway station at Bath Green Park.

With a nice clean train of Mark 2a coaches, D1062 *Western Courier* arrives over the elevated approach to Bath Spa station on the 13.31 service to Paddington.

At Swindon station D1062 *Western Courier* receives the attention of some youthful trainspotters. No doubt the driver is explaining 'No, you cannot all "cab" the loco before it departs!' Swindon station was opened in 1842. The town became home to the well-known Swindon Works, which now houses the STEAM Museum of the Great Western Railway.

Warship diesel hydraulic D854 *Tiger* attracts the attention of some young trainspotters as it awaits the guard's whistle at Reading General before setting off for Paddington. The first coach appears to be a Cravens experimental prototype first class vehicle dating from the late 1950s. It has a black and yellow waist-level bodyside destination or information board.

Western diesel hydraulic, D1067 *Western Druid*, speeds through Reading General towards Paddington on the centre relief line. She is in charge of the prestigious 'Cornish Riviera Express' formed of a tidy train of Mark 1 coaches. A Southern Region 4COR EMU creeps into the picture on the left.

A Pressed Steel single-car DMU W55032 ticks over on arrival at Bridport on 14 August 1971. Bridport station opened in 1857 and the extension to Bridport Harbour, named West Bay by the publicity-conscious Great Western Railway, was opened in 1884.

Slowly entering Cardiff General station with an inter-regional train destined for the Eastern Region is Peak diesel, D43. The station opened in 1850 and was renamed Cardiff Central in 1973, not long after this picture was taken. Following the demise of the coal and steel industries of South Wales and the growth of office accommodation, it is now the busiest station in Wales.

Brush Type 4 no. 1638 waits at Swansea along with a good display of Great Western Railway bracket signals on 6 November 1971. Opened in 1850 the station was previously known as Swansea High Street, to differentiate it from Swansea Victoria, the former London North Western Railway station closed in 1964.

From a passing train an industrial diesel shunter is seen in the steelworks at Llanelli on 6 November 1971.

Hymek D7001 in blue livery is seen at Worcester Shrub Hill on 12 August 1972 having worked in on a service from Paddington. Note the lovely GWR bracket signal. A Sulzer Type 2 and a Brush Type 4 can be seen stabled in the distance.

A Metro-Cammell DMU is seen on arrival at Hereford station from Worcester on 12 August 1972.

As it arrives at Birmingham New Street station on 12 August 1972, Hymek diesel hydraulic loco D7081 in Rail Blue livery catches the attention of some platform-end enthusiasts.

The end of the line. D1002 *Western Explorer* in tandem with another unidentified Western waits departure at Penzance in May 1973 with the 12.20 to Paddington. This picture shows the extent of facilities provided in the relatively small reclaimed area at Penzance station, with a Brush Type 4 and a Sulzer Type 2 either side of the parcels platform in the background.

A closer view of D1002 *Western Explorer* gently ticking over at Penzance.

Seen arriving at Exeter St David's station is a Western with a train of Mark 2 stock on the 07.30 from Paddington to Penzance.

Another Western arrives at Exeter St David's, this time on the 08.36 Cardiff to Paignton service. Note the beautiful sets of Great Western gantry signals on the far platform.

A Brush Type 4 leans to the curve as she heads up towards Exeter St David's on the sea wall at Eastcliffe Bridge, Teignmouth. The lattice spans of this bridge were made in Swindon Works during the 1880s.

The 09.30 Paddington to Penzance service is in the charge of a Western as it heads west along the South Devon sea wall at Eastcliffe, approaching Teignmouth.

Accelerating round the curve under Eastcliffe Bridge towards Exeter St David's is a Peak diesel on the 11.20 Plymouth to Manchester Piccadilly inter-regional service.

Dawlish station sees a Peak leaving past Marine Parade on a westbound Newcastle to Paignton inter-regional train.

A Brush Type 4 in green livery with yellow cab window surrounds emerges from Kennaway Tunnel alongside the Marine Parade and heads towards Dawlish station hauling an eastbound Motorail service. The Motorail brand was introduced in 1966 for the public car-carrying service but gradually phased out by 1995 with the advent of privatisation.

The beach is empty as another Peak heads east towards Exeter. The view was taken from a footbridge at the eastern end of Dawlish station.

A Western awaits departure westwards from Newton Abbot station on the 10.56 Paddington to Penzance service. A Restaurant Car and a Sleeping Car can be seen in the down-side sidings awaiting their next turn of duty.

With the wonderful semaphore signal gantry and the old signal box behind, another Western arrives at Exeter St David's from the west. The lines to the Southern Railway Exeter Central station lead up the 1 in 37 curved gradient on the left, which in steam days required the assistance of banking engines.

A Western with a down train of Mark 2 stock arrives at Reading General. On the right at platform 4a, awaiting departure for Waterloo is the Southern Region's new order in the form of one of the brand new but outdated Mark 1 bodyshell 4CIG EMUs, replacing the elderly 4CORs.

As well as being host to Southern Region EMU trains to Waterloo, platform 4a at Reading General also served the Guildford, Redhill and Tonbridge service. This was worked by a small number of Class 3R 500 hp DEMUs introduced in 1964 and informally known as 'Tadpole' units. They were so called because they were formed from a standard width 64-foot electric trailer coach (the 'body') and two 58-foot narrow-bodied Hastings line carriages (the 'tail'). 3R unit 1204 is seen here arriving.

At the other end of Reading General station the service to Basingstoke arrives and departs. This service, waiting to leave Basingstoke for Reading General, is formed of 3H 600 hp Hampshire DEMUs with 1133 leading. Basingstoke originally had distinct LSWR and GWR stations side by side and this service uses the old GWR platform.

A Peak diesel loco with a train of Mark 1 stock glides over Hayle Viaduct in Cornwall as it heads for Penzance. Harvey's famous foundry was established in Hayle in 1779, reaching its peak in the mid-nineteenth century. It was well-known for producing beam engines for the famous Cornish tin and copper mines, and also exported beam engines worldwide.

Expectant passengers wait as a Brush Type 4 arrives at the cathedral city of Truro with a service for Paddington. The Falmouth branch line operates to and from the bay platform on the far left, while in the background industrial units occupy the area where Truro locomotive shed used to be located. Truro station opened in 1859 and is 301 miles from Paddington.

A DMU on the Truro–Falmouth shuttle service arrives at Falmouth Town station. It was opened in 1970 as Falmouth using components from the closed Perranporth Beach Halt and later renamed The Dell. The branch was built to the broad gauge, opened in 1863, and was converted to standard gauge in 1892. The line was cut back from Falmouth Docks station to here in the 1960s but now runs through to the docks station again. The branch is well promoted and continues to serve the local community and holidaymakers alike.

With the 1960s road bridge behind, a Western leaves Cornwall and enters Devon as it comes slowly over the Royal Albert Bridge, Saltash, on a train to Paddington. Since this picture was taken the walkways on the end towers of the Royal Albert Bridge have been cleared away to present a much tidier appearance. The bridge, designed by Isambard Kingdom Brunel, spans the River Tamar, and dates from 1859.

Western Region three-car Cross Country DMUs on services between Weymouth and Bristol Temple Meads pass at Maiden Newton station. This is situated between Dorchester West and Yeovil Pen Mill and was the junction for the Bridport branch from its opening in 1857 until closure of the branch in 1975.

The end of this book and the end of the line. At Bridport, by this time a single-track terminus, a Pressed Steel single-unit railcar idles awaiting its return journey to Maiden Newton. Judging by the number of people in attendance it must have been around the time closure of the Bridport branch was due to take place on 5 May 1975. The buffer stop in the foreground marks where the branch to West Bay used to continue until it closed in 1930.